Classroom Management Techniques That Work

How to avoid the 55 BIG mistakes that are costing teachers results, stress and missed opportunities!

By David Hyner fpsa alam

& numerous expert guest authors

www.stretchdevelopment.com
www.davidhyner.com
www.goalsettingaudio.com

The content of this book is intended as a guide to improve teacher performance for the benefit of children, teenagers and young adults. It is the collective work of numerous teachers, speakers and trainers who work in the education sector. Before introducing any content within a classroom please ensure that it is a correct fit for your school, both legally and morally and in keeping with the schools rules. Any opinions expressed by individual authors are not necessarily the opinion of David Hyner or Stretch Development Ltd.

Huge thanks to all co-authors who collaborated on this venture.

About the lead author:
David Hyner (fpsa) of Stretch Development Ltd

David has worked in schools all over England giving keynote talks and workshops to between 20,000 and 50,000 students and teachers each year.

In that time he has seen thousands of teachers interacting with students, parents and fellow professionals.

David is a renowned professional speaker and in this book he gives you the "MUST AVOID" list of the 55 BIG mistakes made by some teachers

and ....how **YOU can avoid unwittingly doing them yourself.**

David Hyner and a range of experienced teachers, trainers and speakers (credited alongside the Mistake they have written) have contributed to this book with the first 20 "BIG Mistakes" written by David himself.

This book gives you simple, easy to apply, effective solutions to improved classroom management. It's based on many years of research into how highly effective teachers, trainers, speakers and presenters work.

This gives you increased confidence, certainty and conviction to be the teacher that is remembered for all the right reasons.

David delivers workshops and talks on the subject of personal effectiveness including:

Independent learning, Goal Setting, Confidence, Memory Skills, Revision Skills, Motivation, Presentation Skills, Enterprise Events, AimHigher, Attitude, Adventures, Communications, Emotional Intelligence, Gifted & Talented, Int. Skills, Fundraising, Team Building, Stress, Body Language, Personal Responsibility.

Plus: Stretch associates include many inspiring professional speakers and top achievers that can visit your school to share their message.

The tips and advice given within these pages are not guaranteed to work for every teacher as everyone has their own unique style of working. They are, however, based upon tried and tested

techniques that David and the contributors have
seen used by successful and effective teachers,
and/or used by them to aid control, discipline
and improve class/group management.

BIG Mistake No 1: No Rules Teaching

Many teachers believe that "school rules" are enough to keep order and/or inspire students to be at their best. I have seen many schools where this works but there are others where discipline gets way out of hand. Classroom rules laid in stone during the first few lessons can help avoid this.

At the beginning of the school year ask students what they want to achieve and what they believe is acceptable and unacceptable behaviour within the classroom if this is to be achieved. Get them to write it all down. This can include how they have to "be" or "behave" in your lessons. This may include, start on time, respect opinions and people, silence when requested, homework on time etc. Get students discussing what are the key things that they can agree on that are to be "the class rules" for YOUR lessons.

Students should then **ALL agree** that for as long

as you deliver their learning outcomes, that they will follow their rules. Agree a consequence criteria and reward structure that is fun, acceptable to all, and enforceable (that may follow the school discipline code … or not). I have seen water pistol punishments, chocolate bar rewards, un-cool nicknames used for a day both as rewards and punishments. Get these "class rules" drawn up nicely, laminate them and stick on the wall during lessons where all can see.

You may find that lesson discipline is a self-governing thing for a long period of time. Situations that may have escalated quickly are now sorted and dealt with by pointing to the rules and asking an unruly student "do you and the class think that your rules are being stuck to?"

BIG Mistake No 2: Looks Really Can Kill

It is often said that people can tell what another is thinking or feeling just by their facial expression. Didn't somebody once say, "the eyes are the window to the soul"?

So can you remember a teacher from your schooldays that had a face like thunder...........? Remember the one with "that" reputation?

Facial expression and good eye contact can engage trust like little else can.

Have you ever seen those friendly "meeters and greeters" in your local large supermarket? They're the ones with the big badge saying "Ask Me" and the brightly coloured tabard or jacket!

Is this just for customer relationships do you think?

No .... They do it because study suggests that if eye contact is made with someone as they enter the store, the shopper is less likely to steal because they both feel a connection with the store staff and/or they think they will be seen.

What can we take from this as teaching professionals?

Stand either at the door or at the front as students walk into the room and even if they do not look at you, make eye contact with each and every student as they enter the room.

Verbally acknowledge the students as they enter with a "hello…. How are you?" (Or another greeting.)

Sounds simplistic doesn't it? But think about it...

If you went to buy a second hand car and the seller would not look you in the eye. He or she then told you of its "one owner who was an old dear who used the motor to run down the shops". Would you buy that car from them? ….. I think not?

Sincerity is "KEY" here. Do not do this (or most of what is in this book) if you do not "mean" it with good intent. It will reflect it in your body language and then it will be seen as fake and others will then not trust you.

BIG Mistake No 3: The Famine In The Classroom

A smile costs nothing yet gives so much.

Up front I must state (as with eye contact) that if you are not sincere with your actions here, then a fake can be spotted very easily by students. Be sure to "mean" what you do and say to young adults.

For some great teachers there is fun, smiling and enjoyment built into the lesson plan for each and every session. For others it can seem that each lesson is a trudge through the day without any hint of fun or enjoyment.

Why?........ There doesn't have to be a famine of smiles!

A smile can be infectious (in a groovy way!) and as a welcome. When combined with good eye contact, smiling can build rapport quicker than anything else.

As an icebreaker, get students (or teachers) to sit

and face the front. Connect emotionally with an authentic thought and feeling of love, appreciation and happiness as you look each student in the eye.

Your natural smile (and grin) will receive an almost instant reciprocation from most. In fact, for someone to resist smiling back at you would take a good deal of willpower - which you can even acknowledge as a skill.

It is hardwired into our brain as an automatic response as a baby to mimic a smile (with the exception of those who were not smiled at as a child of course ?!?!)

Smiling and delivering a happy classroom environment can become a habit that pays dividends long into the school year. Students will "want "to attend your lessons and remember you as a "cool teacher" for all the right reasons.

I bet you can remember at least one teacher who engaged you and held your attention through such methods.

BIG Mistake No 4: Not Gaining Trust

You will not believe, or at best "not listen", to a teacher that you do not trust.
Many things can help gain or improve trust. But to start with, when combined with eye contact and a genuine smile, a simple handshake can build trust over time.

In this short book I can sadlynot go into great depth on this subject but here are a few tips to help teaching professionals.

The handshake should be a greeting to or for another person:
- NOT a way of showing others how strong you are
- NOT an awkward thing you do whilst avoiding eye contact and looking at the floor giving a limp wristed apology for a handshake
- NOT a high five, punch fist or other "street" greeting in a vain attempt at getting credibility with young adults. (I tried that and got laughed out the room)

Look others in the eye. Smile and offer a hand that is straight. (Not up, exposing the palm, or down showing the top of the hand.)

Put your hand in theirs and match their grip intensity as this shows an attempt at rapport. If your handshake is "too" different it can break rapport as easily as gain it.

Stand at the doorway as they enter the room or at the front and ask them all to shake hands as they enter. This, despite initial embarrassment or potential ridicule, can quickly become something that bonds you with students as they will assume that you are treating them with respect and as an adult.

Top Tip
If they offer you an 'open' palm handshake that is weak then gently turn their hand level, keep eye contact and smile. An open palm combined with lack of eye contact and awkward body language 'can' (not always) suggest a lack of confidence in the other person. By turning their hand level you are telling them that you treat them as an equal.

If they offer you their hand 'on top' with palm

faced down this 'can' (again…. not always) suggest that they assume or seek dominance in the relationship. It's vital that you, again, smile and look them in the eye while you gently turn their hand level as you shake hands. This helps in showing them that they are not in control and that you are equals.

If you need to assert yourself, you may even consider turning your hand slightly over theirs as you turn it to show that you are in control in this situation.

BIG Mistake No 5: No Time Management

Again...... a huge subject that I could give you a book on all by itself!

My observations have suggested that there are two reasons why some teachers struggle with time.

1) They have not planned and controlled the lesson
2) Students have controlled the lesson

Most human beings (especially at the start of a new experience, such as a new class at the start of a year) seek to be guided as to the rules, structure and general feel for what is happening.

Try these ....

a) If you have a 50 minute lesson, allow five to ten minutes at the end for the "teach me" section. This is where the students have to teach the teacher what they have learnt in the lesson. After all, do we not

15

learn best when we teach?

b) Give students clear outlines of how time is going by having a piece of music on a loop playing during your lesson. The music is the exact length of your lesson. It begins at a normal/louder level and gets quieter over a 90 second period to silence. This gives students a clear (and agreed) sign that the lesson is starting. You can have a mid-lesson piece of music if you wish to serve as a reminder to yourself and make sure you are on target with your lesson plan. Then, at the end the 90 second loop gets louder giving students a clear sign that the lesson is or has finished.

c) Between the start and end loops of music, you can have a piece of baroque music playing at a barely audible level which is said to help students with concentration levels.

Another great time management tip is to think about what you do at lunchtime.
Sure, the staff room can offer some light relief from the daily routine but is it serving you or hindering you?

Is the conversation positive and upbeat? If so then keep going. If not, try going for a five or ten minute brisk walk, or get some fresh air whilst eating your sandwich. Then close the classroom door and get some marking or planning done. Thirty minutes saved each day that you could use relaxing of an evening instead?

Worth a try eh?

BIG Mistake No 6: Not Knowing How To Open & Close A Lesson

Take just a minute or two at the start of each lesson to let the students understand what it is they will be doing in your lesson. This pre-frames their mind to be more accepting of what they are about to hear or experience.

Perhaps MORE importantly, talk to them (rather than "telling" them) "WHY" they should listen and learn this information. Give them the benefits, to them, of knowing and retaining this information so that they have a term of reference or reason to get involved.

Refer to your introduction;
"As we said at the start, we are now going to learn ………. So that you can ……….. Which gives you the ability to ………."

Would you be more motivated if you understood the benefit and outcomes of your work?

I recall a great teacher from when I was a student that had a fearsome reputation, yet had the respect of students because of the way he ran his lesson.

Mr.Dyson made it very clear what was and what was not acceptable behaviour in his lesson. If the lesson had gone well he would get us to put our books away about five minutes before the end and he would sit on the front of his desk and chat to us like adults. He asked our opinions and enquired about our hobbies, interests and "take" on things ranging from school, current affairs or other (sometimes close to the knuckle) subjects that were of concern or interest to us.

Because we knew where we stood with him;
Because he treated us like adults;
Because he listened and took interest;

…….. he was labelled as a "cool teacher".

Even the tough kids respected him.

BIG Mistake No 7: Lack Of Visibility

Some teachers wonder why some students do not treat them with respect or ask questions?

Being "there" for students when they need us is key to this.

If "every" lunchtime and break you seek the sanctuary of the staff room and "tut" at the thought of giving your time up for students, I beg you to think again.

As human beings we naturally trust and respect (more) those who are visible as being "there" for us. There when needed and/or those who we know where they will be if we needed them.

Do your students know where to find you or how to approach you if they needed to?

What if you as a professional were more visible in the corridors in-between lessons? It raises your profile and reputation amongst the student body and also acts as a preventative approach to behaviour issues in break times.

One school saw a MASSIVE turnaround in behaviour as a result of teachers all agreeing to take this approach as part of a series of measures to aid student attitude.

Then, at lesson time, be at your classroom or lecture theatre before your students. Be visible in the doorway (which will improve behaviour in the corridor vicinity). It also plays a part as the start of a greeting to your class.......

Maybe before you shake their hands and make eye contact whilst smiling as they enter the classroom?............... just a thought!

And finally I would strongly advocate being visible in places and at times where "your" students least expect you to appear.

If whilst in conversation you discover that a few of your students are in the hockey or rugby team, or they are part of an enterprise group that is starting a business to raise money for charity......... why not turn up and support them just because you "give a stuff" ?!

The smallest things can make the BIGGEST

differences!

Be visible, be heard, be known and be seen.

BIG Mistake No 8: Lack Of Praise

This is all about being consistent.

Be consistent in your use of praise and your discipline.

Many "middle of the road" students are only in need of appropriate praise and encouragement to achieve at a higher level.

Regardless of how you manage the classroom your ability to get students to listen, engage and respond to you will increase if - from the start - you are perceived as being firm, fair and consistent with praise and discipline.

In relation to praise….. it costs nothing but a tiny amount of energy and concentration to pounce on positives when they happen.

Each and every time a student does or says ANYTHING positive, pounce on it and give sincere praise. Again….. a fake will be spotted a mile off so don't go here unless you "mean it"

If a student has made even the slightest effort to take themselves to the next level, it is essential to support them, re-enforce their ability and if required, hold them accountable.

When giving praise it is great to point at the person and speak with conviction as you say "well done...." (Oh ... I can hear my mother now saying that it is rude to point at people!)

Do not be afraid to use body language to emphasise praise by taking a step towards them and leaning slightly towards the student at which you are directing the praise.

Ask students to rate, or even score, success within the group or by individuals as this raises awareness of others within the group who could otherwise become "grey" students.

Have celebrations specific to your classes where, for example, if the group work together to revise and can score an average of XXXXX in the next test or exam, you will reward them with XXXXX?

BIG Mistake No 9: Shouting & Raising The Voice

I was about to start a keynote/workshop to a year 11 group, 240 in number and had opened my mouth to begin speaking when ....

The noise was incredible!

A teacher that I had talked with just ten minutes earlier in a calm and fun conversation was standing outside the hall berating a student on the top of his voice. The student had a facial expression that screamed "WHAT- EVER !" Yet, the teacher persisted in his torrent (and volume) of finger pointing and red faced rage.

Who came out on top in that situation?

I have had a knife pulled on me, had a student swear at me and walk out, had a student threaten to "blast the flesh from the Zionist" and even had one refuse to say single word throughout. (I didn't even know what a Zionist was at the time. I had to look it up! …… I am not one.)

Each of these situations was dealt with to a satisfactory conclusion without me even raising my voice.

Would you "EVER" be inspired to achieve or change any behaviour by someone shouting at you in such a tone?

So why do we do it?

Warning

Anyone who does the above may not like what I am about to tell you…….

People shout at young adults because they lack the skills to control, motivate or discipline without having to resort to a sense of superiority that is unfair when used against a developing mind.

This statement may sound a bit severe, but be honest with yourself……….. Have you ever respected someone who has shouted at you?

"IF" you know the student well (and/or understand their mindset) and they have let themselves down in any way, it (in my experience) can have a far better effect if you ask them (not shout) a question such as: "Is that acceptable to you, bearing in mind what you are capable of?"

BIG Mistake No 10: Not Delivering The Goods

If your employer promised to back you in a dispute with a parent or student where you were in the right?
If your employer were to promise you improved conditions of work?
If the government were to promise you a pay rise or a new build school?
……. And then not deliver……

Would you believe another word they said to you?

… EVER ?!

So, if you promise students one thing and then don't deliver how can we expect any rapport, reputation or acceptance afterwards?
Would you expect them to engage with you and learn in your lessons?
The customer service mantra holds true: "Under Promise & Over Deliver!"

If you are to improve your performance as

teacher you must do what you say you are going to do.

If you promise rewards – follow through.

If you threaten discipline – follow through if required.

If you promise anything ……. Follow through …. Or in those situations where you may *have* to break a promise……..Make it up to them.

BIG Mistake No 11: Lack Of Profile & Reputation

How many times have you seen it happen?

Two teachers go for the same job promotion.
Both equally capable.
If anything you get slightly better results. The other teacher gets the job because of what you perceive as being "more popular, or having been there longer"

Or………

A student is working on a project and needs help or support with it in an area that you can help with. Frustratingly you watch the student (despite your verbal offers of help) ask parents and tutors for advice but not yourself resulting in the student handing in a piece of work that could have been so much better.

Reputation can be confused with egotism, and many other things that hold a negative connotation and a bad (even if wrongly assumed) reputation can spread ten times faster within any community than any good or positive reputation.

Go the extra mile, help students, get involved, talk to them, and understand them. Do the same with your fellow teachers.
Whilst it's important that you hold a good reputation with your fellow professionals, it is your relationship, rapport and reputation with the student body and their parents that will raise your reputation quicker than anything else. You could be remembered as the "cool teacher"!

At times where you may feel under pressure to do "things right" your reputation longer term will be better served by doing the "right thing"

Reputation improves when you speak to young adults as if they were adults.

Work on emotional intelligence and communication skills. Invest in yourself and your skill set. Try an NLP (Neuro Linguistic Programming) workshop or book to understand more about language, tonality and how to use it to influence and gain rapport. Read a book on body language, stress prevention, or understand how to empathise more. Increasingly, we are seeing more and more young people in our schools with issues around self esteem, confidence or using inappropriate behaviour that masks things going on outside of the school gates.

Be authentic, be there, be positive and be supportive. Your reputation will grow for all the right reasons.

BIG Mistake No 12: Little Or No Rapport

"Who are you?"
"Why should I listen to you?"
"I don't really care what you're telling me!"

If you have heard these things, or have ever seen a "look" on a face that suggests they may be thinking any of the above, then it could be because a teacher or parent is trying to give information, learning, or asking a request of a student before they have gained a rapport with them.

As adults we do it all the time as well. I have seen many a senior leader (on staff training days that I deliver) "tell" of big changes that "will" be implemented before they have got rapport with their team.

In our two hour workshops on goal setting, revision skills, enterprise or presentation skills we can spend up to the first 15-30 minutes engaging the audience while seeking rapport and permission to work with them.

Without this, asking them to try anything new or potentially challenging is a real issue. This is where a great introduction (including rules, incentives, consequences and fun) can actually win over potentially disruptive students from the off and even get them on your side.

When we work with students we ask up front:

- "I want to speak to you like adults today. Is it okay with you if I do this?"
- "If you stay, take part and have fun I promise you that there is a chance of winning XXXXXXXX and I will give you 100% and respect you totally."
- "If you decide to stay in the room then mess around you accept these consequences XXXXXXXXXXXXX"
- "If you do not agree to the rules, you can come right now and shake my hand and I will respect that you have made an adult decision. I will allow you to sit at the side and not take part. But if you then doss around, you will be subject to the same consequences as the rest of them."
- "What is acceptable and unacceptable behaviour? How do we need to "be" and "behave" to get the most from this

session?

I have even been known to burn some money, do a magic trick, give away a prize up front with the promise of more for those who "step up" at the start. This is to engage the audience enabling me to then give them information that is then more readily taken in and accepted. I use self effacing humour to show that I am not scared of what others say or think about me, which again can let the more challenging students know that I am not weak and I do what I say.

The trick is to treat them like adults unless they deserve otherwise.

BIG Mistake No 13: Little Or "NO" Recap Of Work

It is vital to recap or review your work with student to ensure that their retention and recall of information is at the right level to achieve what you need them to do.

Rather than do a dry and potentially boring, revision session, have a go at using a memory technique that links your information to silly, scary and fun images.

Your lesson start can be you teaching the students a silly or fun list of things that link to the key points of your lesson. Then, at the end, you can recall the list with them and explain during the lesson how each image links to a key learning point.

If done correctly, you will find that students will happily want to try and recall your lists over time and if done with real flair they will be able to recall amazing amounts of information just by using these image lists.

A German psychologist called Hermann Ebbinghaus (well worth looking into) did extensive work on memory and recall and habitual thinking and behaviour. He proved that over time, if work is recalled and reviewed, both the recall and comprehension of information rose drastically.

Mind mapping, memory stacking, memory journey and many other memory and accelerated learning techniques can take very little time to learn and can get rapport (due to it being fun) with students and can have a MASSIVE impact on your results.

Get students out of the classroom and take them for a short walk around the school as you recall out aloud the key points of a lesson, maybe to a tune, or rhyme.

Using the above mentioned techniques I once did an experiment in a primary school and taught an A level history piece using a fun story and a memory stacking technique.

Within 40 minutes "ALL" students could recall twenty facts about ancient Egypt and explain to a teachers satisfaction that they had a grasp of the context and application of these facts.

One day, we may even see closed eye relaxation processes with subliminal teaching used to aid recall. My own initial experiments with this have shown some impressive results.

BIG Mistake No 14: Lack Of Personal And Professional Development

"What a waste of time"
"I don't need to learn new things"
"Fluffy woolly nonsense"

Frequent expressions heard in relation to personal and professional development.

"I did my teaching degree, what else do I need?" is perhaps the most common one I have heard. This attitude may enable you to get your head down and "get some work done". However, it can be a little short sighted and can greatly inhibit your effectiveness as a teaching professional in the longer term. It can also limit your chances of promotion and advancement. At the very least it may lead to a "reputation" of being close minded, negative in mindset, aloof, or even not part of the team.

If you are a dedicated professional I can suggest three things that can change/improve your skills, reputation and effectiveness.

1) Looking into

I once interviewed Gold medal athlete Kriss Akabusi who said that if somebody was good at something you wanted to be good at, you should look "into" them rather than "up-to" them.

He suggested that we should study how they do what it is they do in fine detail. Preparation, delivery, stance, voice, gesture, thoughts and behaviours...... We should then model these and make them our own.

2) Reading & selective course attendance

Read the latest ideas from leading thinkers, teachers and business gurus. Attend courses and workshops but be sure to know 100% what you will take from it and apply. Never just turn up, learn, leave, then use nothing.

3) Own time investment

The serious and ambitious teacher may even invest in themselves in their own time. I would strongly recommend learning about

body language, personality profiling, NLP
(Neuro Linguistic Programming), coaching
skills, mentoring skills etc

BIG Mistake No 15: Being Too Serious & Over Use Of The Stick

It is important to remember that a teacher's main focus is, or should be, student development and academic results.

Huge pressures are placed on teachers by the curriculum, parents, leadership, government and themselves. Add to this the workday that seems controlled by a bell and you could easily be forgiven for having periods of time where you lose sight of "why" you came into teaching.

For many it is to "make a difference" to the lives of young people.

I frequently see teachers at the point of burn out either through workload, bad time management or stress.

A straight face is common. A frown is frequently seen. I have even seen scowls from time to time. Once I saw a student receiving a "hair drying" screaming barrage from a teacher for very little reason. Maybe you know someone who takes their frustrations out on students?

STOP !! ....

Before it gets to this point focus on how you can personally be happier at work. Smile more. Make time for fun in the classroom.

Give the students (and yourself) incentives and rewards for excellent work and really "stepping up".

There can be no benchmark for how many times it is acceptable - or not - to shout at a young adult. I would say only in praise, or if you felt personally threatened.

If you're shouting or raising your voice in anger more than a couple of times a month then maybe you need to look at your style of managing situations. Perhaps consider some training in conflict resolution and communication skills.

I took offence when someone suggested that I should learn about communication skills etc, but what I learnt and applied has helped me to successfully manage groups of 240 students for anything from one hour up to a whole day.

Look for positives in your students, especially those who seem to be always on the end of your wrath. Ask them for their side of a situation and listen to them to make sure that your version is the true one, as it is not always the case.

BIG Mistake No 16: Lines Drawn In Sand

"I told you that if you did that again you would
be out the classroom!!!"
"Once more and I mean it!"

Have you ever caught yourself saying that?

It is very hard to take someone at their word if
they draw lines in sand. By that I mean that if
you say you will do one thing and then do
another you will lose respect very quickly.

The start of a year, or first few lessons with a
new group, is critical to set boundaries enabling
student to know what they can and can't do.
Also, what the consequences will be if they
continue with disruptive behaviour.

If you have students with attention issues or
behavioural challenges get them on your side by
asking them to be a group leader or director and
govern behaviour. Choose students for tasks on
the condition that they themselves work to the
guidelines agreed or set out in a lesson.

There are a few people who thrive on being in control of a situation but in group settings - whether they are students, teachers or parents - most people (in a new situation) seek to be led and told what to do.

I once took a group of business leaders on an adventure experience. These people were all business owners or senior leaders who were very capable of managing people and situations that they are familiar with. I stood back and watched them as we arrived in our foreign and rural location where they knew no language or plan of what to do.

They became almost children, looking for a leader or assuming to be a leader. In some cases they showed big signs of stress at being out of their comfort zones by saying and doing things that they would have found unthinkable back home. As soon as we took control and guided them, they were fine again.

Have you ever seen this in a teacher's staffroom discussion or a student group? Therefore is it any wonder that in a lesson, if the teacher does not assert themselves as being in control, then they will seek take control?

Be the boss and draw lines in stone, not sand.
Do what you say you will do.

By all means be open to opinions and be fair, but
there should always be lines that are not
crossed.
And if they are ....?
Know and rehearse exactly what you will do in
that situation.

BIG Mistake No 17: Not Using The Biggest Weapon In The Teacher's Armoury

For the sake of this piece I will refer to the "weapon" as "Ryan".
Every class has one.......... A "Ryan".

Ryan is a nice lad who has a short attention span.

He is the tough cookie that may even be feared by his peers.

He is quite smart but hides it very well behind a lack of self esteem and the wrong peer group.

He is not "nasty" but is always seeking to challenge, disrupt or be silly without invitation or provocation.

One to one he is great, but in front of his mates he becomes the "ring leader".

Know him do you? How many do you have in your classes?

Speak to Ryan and, if possible, his parents. Use very passionate and positive language and tonality to say that you want to help him and will stand by him if he does right. Use gestures and body language to express how serious you are using positive language all the time.

Ask Ryan to help you by influencing his friends in a positive way. Ask for support and permission from Ryan and his parents to use incentives and consequences should Ryan tow the line and get involved, or step over the line and do wrong.

In class, if Ryan does anything (and I do mean "anything" positive) pounce on it and re-affirm the positive with "well done", "great contribution" etc

Use Ryan as an example to other potentially unruly students by pointing out how good Ryan is being and how they could learn from him.

If Ryan steps out of line, use the consequences agreed with parents. When he succeeds be sure to follow through with the agreed reward.

BIG Mistake No 18: An Expedition Without A Compass

Having your own lesson plans and target grades are all well and good, but do you ever seek opinion from the students both as individuals and as a class on setting their own targets?

If you are teacher and you have "say" 24 students in your group, would it be wise to set out on a trek with only you holding a compass and knowing how to use it?

Goal setting is key and, if used correctly, can be a superb motivator for young adults.

I strongly advocate that you take time early in the year to set goals with the group and update them on their progress each lesson.

Frequently a group will motivate themselves to up their grades as the spirit of competition takes over.

Draw a plan and timeline so that students can easily see where they are in relation to their progress and understand if they are on target or not.

A plan or target that has the students "buy in" will always be received better than one that is set by the teacher alone
.

Constant review, praise and support is needed but the results are well worth the effort.

This can also serve as a motivator to you as a momentum can be built and maintained over the course of the year.

BIG goals can be perceived as setting some students up for a fall. In my experience, with the right support, they can achieve things that are massive strides forward for them.

Look at http://www.goalsettingaudio.com

BIG Mistake No 19: The Samaritan Principle

A good Samaritan is needed by us all from time to time. A real Samaritan though will do the right thing, even if at times it's at the expense of doing things right.

The best Samaritan is one who's not afraid to say or do what is right - even if it is perceived by the recipient as being unhelpful. As long as the Samaritan KNOWS that it is helpful.

A great teacher will support a student in stretching themselves and hold them accountable when times are tough.

They will push, support, motivate, inspire .... and educate students to achieve. But, when times get tough, they are not afraid to say what needs to be said in a supportive manner.

Check in with students both as a group and one to one to see what they are struggling with. Hold a brainstorming session with the group to get ideas on how each of the class members can overcome their challenge/s.

This teaches problem solving, independent learning and confidence.

If a student is struggling with algebra in maths, a brainstorm within the group can be made fun and inter-active. "They" come up with ideas and answers as to how the student could overcome their hurdle. This way they are more likely to take action as the answer has come from their peers rather than "the teacher".

Having said this, the Samaritan teacher is also open to change and is quick to change opinion and even offer an apology (yes ….. a genuine one) if he or she is proven to have been wrong.

BIG Mistake No 20: Lack Of Emotional Intelligence

This can be one of the most far reaching mistakes. Teaching professionals who do not pay attention to this can experience consequences that reach far beyond the classroom. I talk of your own health, energy levels and stress prevention.

Notice that I said stress "prevention" and not management?

Having interviewed many leading psychologists, neuroscientists, emotional and intelligence experts I offer the following advice. Know that without addressing your health, levels of energy and/or stress that you can be limiting your professional effectiveness, your personal wellbeing, and even your domestic personal life and relationships at home.

Please …….. take action.

Do you work, eat and sleep? Or, do you build

sections of your day and week that are set aside for "you". It could be sport, massage, relaxation, walking, comedy, meditation, hobbies etc, Have something that is set into your diary that, whenever possible, is an unmovable diary feature. In a teachers line of work it can be too easy to just "get on with it" and pay little attention to yourself.

Put your life vest on first!

That is what they say on the in-flight emergency card. How can you best serve young people, yourself or your family if you are not first in a position of good health, happiness and wellbeing?

Do things that make you happy. Wear a smile.

Begin by identifying what areas of your life cause you the most stress. This can be different for many people. It could be a threat of emotional or physical danger as with a fire fighter or A&E nurse. It may be travelling stress where you have issues at work and you take the issue out on the people at home or vice versa.

Maybe there is clash of leadership styles or personalities, or maybe it is workload and/or time management. Either way, if you know what is causing you your stress you can then look at the situation and ask the following powerful question:

In this situation which one, two (or all) of the following is something that I either fear a lack of, or desire more of?

Security
Control
Acceptance

In every stressful situation as human beings we seek either more of these, or fear the lack of them. It may be just one of these, two of these or at times, all three.

If you identify this it is easier for our logical minds to find options and solutions rather than being paralysed by fear when you cannot think how you can overcome your stress.

When I work with teachers on stress prevention the most common fear and stressor tends to be government inspections.

What is it you fear a lack of, or desire more of, in this situation?

For each individual it could be a different answer.

Maybe you would not feel in control if an assessor was in the room? Maybe your personal security would be threatened if you were sacked? Maybe it would be the lack of acceptance from your peer group if you failed?

Either way, you can then take steps to overcome this stress. In my experience most teachers are EXCELLENT at their job when they just get out of their own way and teach to the best of their ability.

If you are being the very best you can be, then the only thing any assessor could offer you is constructive critique and who on earth wouldn't want ideas that could make them even better?

My approach is to treat assessors as the biggest kid in the room who is more in need of your lesson than any other student.

BIG Mistake No 21:
Appearing perfect

Joy Marsden
Speaker and trainer
http://www. joymarsdem.com

Whilst I am not advocating that teachers bare all
their weaknesses, the impression teachers
sometimes give to their students is that they
themselves never had a challenge to overcome.

The human race is full of stories of people who
have tried something, felt the challenge and
failed. More importantly, those who have
learned from their failures have gone on to
achieve tremendous things.

Really – no one shrinks back from a story like
this, it only helps to serve those people who are
not yet seeing the results they want to see and
helps them to see that everyone is on a journey -
and that you the teacher is on a journey, just like
them.

It takes real courage to share a personal story of
struggle, and may feel uncomfortable; but doing

this can have long term benefits for both you and the student.

When students know that you are being real with them, they in turn start to become more real with you, making asking for help far more easy.

One school I've been working with in Northampton ran a day of working with a group of underachieving students leading up to their GCSE exams. The day was to follow with a parents evening where I was giving a talk to emphasise all that we had been encouraging the students to do. Up until that point, the current record for parents attending at the parents evening was a low as 3%.
After working with the students all day they encouraged their parents to come and 85% attended.

The difference – The students related to aspects of shared challenge and this not only broke down barriers, but built trust and hope. A massive result for all, as students, parents and teachers sat together throughout the evening, talking through a 12 week plan to help each student achieve their full potential for their exams.

Life isn't perfect, we aren't perfect – sometimes we get things wrong.

Let the students know that you are on a journey – just like them!

BIG Mistake No 22: **Not building a bridge**

Alex Evans
Autism Speaker
www.optimisminautism.co.uk

I was diagnosed with Asperger's syndrome at 13, which means I am on the autistic spectrum. I left mainstream school in 2003 and my experience was that there was not much knowledge of autism and how best to deal with and teach the pupil. Naturally, I was faced with different teaching styles. However, some teachers wanted to learn more about Asperger's and how they could make working with me a more positive and productive partnership. Whereas others didn't want to acknowledge I had special needs and were not prepared to adapt their teaching styles to accommodate my learning.

Address the behaviour NOT the child.

Below are 2 extracts from my school report in Year 9:-
English – "Alex is a conscientious boy who

obviously wants to do well; he has made good progress and always does his best to act on any advice given. He is well organised and homework is always completed."

Geography – "Although I understand the difficulties he faces, Alex has made very little effort and shown little interest which has been frustrating. Nevertheless there can be little excuse for Alex's disgraceful examination result of which he should be thoroughly ashamed. He only succeeded in making himself look rather silly".

Those reports are poles apart; you would believe they are referring to two different pupils. A common thread with people with ASC is that we have a Jekyll and Hyde type character. Although does it depend on how we are taught as to which side of us you will see?

My English teacher treated me as a student full of potential and hard- working and that is who I became.

My geography teacher treated me as an unruly, lazy pupil and that is who I became. His solution was to isolate me from the rest of the class. Was it any wonder I flunked my examination?

The best way to teach somebody with autism is with positivity! Engage with them, do NOT isolate!! We can never have enough PRAISE when we are working well which in turn will BOOST our self-esteem and raise our confidence levels. Then, we are more inclined to LISTEN and be motivated to SUCCEED. These MINOR alterations can have a tremendous effect on our learning. If teachers can earn respect and gain our trust, you will see a profound improvement in our co-operation with you.

BIG Mistake No 23: Going it alone

Deborah Hulme
Assistant Headteacher

Don't try to 'go-it-alone'. You can waste hours trying to reinvent the wheel.

This doesn't mean that you can't be creative and innovative but be prepared to use the experience of other colleagues to your benefit - work smart and get yourself a mentor.

Look around at colleagues whose professionalism, presence and/or status you admire or aspire to and ask one of them, from your school or local consortium, to mentor you.

Most colleagues will undertake this role very willingly.

Be sure that when you approach them, you can outline the sort of mentoring support that you would like: occasional email or telephone contact to ask advice on a specific issue, half-termly meetings to review your professional progress and sketch out future plans or the opportunity to watch them teach or to shadow them in some other aspect of their role.

If you do not yet feel ready to take this step, identify a colleague who you feel you can model yourself on. Success in the classroom can often be achieved by modelling others' successful classroom and behaviour management.

BIG Mistake No 24: Not establishing and maintaining teacher authority

Kokila Lane

Ensure that students have entered the classroom appropriately and seat them in a manner that enables everyone to see you and you see everyone. To get attention, you need to give attention: which means eye-contact. A teacher with focus achieves tremendously well in their role. Your focus is your ability to manage the focus of your pupils.

Use this simple and effective technique: Say, politely and firmly, achieving eye-contact with every student: "I will speak to you when I am ready".

Teacher authority is rooted in the teacher's belief in themselves that they are competent teachers. Teachers lacking this self-belief leak out the exact opposite message, non-verbally: I am not competent. Expectation sets is all: these teachers set themselves up to fail. What teachers say contributes 7% towards success; how it is said contributes 38% towards success. 55% of positive impact comes from Non-Verbal Communication.

Positive, open, relaxed, engaged and engaging body language reaps the same from students. Students mirror, or reciprocate, teacher behaviour. If you relate to students in a positive manner, they will relate to you in a positive manner. If you work hard, they will work hard. If you give them 100% of your attention, they will give 100% of their attention. They value teachers who establish authority, maintain authority, are fair and that know how to teach well.

I regularly use the key phrase in classrooms as my teaching gets off to a pace respectful of the need of most students to "get on". "I will speak to you when I am ready".

Many teachers hand over control of time and focus to pupils by answering questions, at the inappropriate time: at the start of a lesson. Not answering pupil's questions at the beginning of your session, but ensuring that you will when you are ready, communicates that:

- you are in charge
- you are taking responsibility
- you have authority

When pupils are adamant that they must speak to you, give them paper and pencil and ask them to write you a brief note. You can process this communication without diverging from your trajectory for students' learning.

You, the teacher, are in charge: accept, develop and enjoy your authority.
Alongside a genuine interest in and respect for students, fair, consistent and low-key assertion of authority is what students want and what they need, from their teachers.

BIG Mistake No 25: Having A High Expectation Of Perfection

Bhagirathi Behera
Principal
Green Valley International School, Pusa

An angry administrator is unable to sit-down calmly in the office. Their frustration is at the highest level due to the unexpected negative result of their staff performing a given task. This is a regular scene and situation for any type of boss in any type of office.

As an administrator, supervisor and principal everybody expects that their staff should complete their work in time, without any error and productive result. But it is very frustrating when they are showing incompetency and irregularity.

As everybody knows: perfect result needs perfect people. Perfection depends upon perfect selection, training, instruction and investment.

But, all staff are coming under the principle of individual difference in respect of education, training, competency, interest, attitude and target on the common goal of organizational growth.

In this situation, supervising regrets their own decision, selection and instruction. As a result they are not at par in terms of investment, in the form of time, money, satisfaction and market value.

Here the mantra is not to focus on the undoubting failures of workers but to give a deep thought on few successful points as:
1. Analyse your own instruction whether it was proper, clear and understandable for everybody in respect of the employee's receiving capacity.
2. Identify the aptitude of every employee and give the task according to their capacity in respect of competency and sincerity.
3. Don't wait for result or have blind faith that teachers will complete their work according to your instruction
4. Never lose heart for incompetency of an employee, instead go for any remedy to improve competency
5. Routine follow up is the best policy to get expected result it means involving yourself

during process instead of after the result.
6.Be strict with negative energy creators because they have the power to change positive employee to negative. It means an obstruction in the process of getting expecting result.
7. Appreciate everybody. Even for small success because it creates confidence and faith towards the boss and the task.

So I would like to conclude with a word that if nobody is perfect in this world so how can we expect or demand perfection from employee. We can improve the productivity of employee in a thought provoking and practical way.

BIG Mistake No 26: Doing everything

Simon Ripley - Headteacher

We all like to please other people, make sure the kids are getting the best from our input and to make a good impression. For teachers this starts during those dizzying days of Teacher Training when we want to shine because we all secretly (or not so secretly) hope a job comes up in a placement we like. The hours are long but we can always find that little bit extra time to do more than we should. Notice me! I'm the one you want for your school! If not I really want a killer reference!

We're like this throughout our lives but never more so than in the bustling environment of a school where literally there are never enough hours in the day. But we keep doing it and I have seen this time and time again. Those who are brilliant at their jobs keep saying yes- for the right reasons undoubtedly- but they keep saying it! As an NQT you have to prove you were 'the right choice'. Then comes the promotion prospects for the ambitious among us. We all know when Mr X is planning on retiring (though he may stay a few more years to thwart our rise to power) and we need to make sure the Head knows who we are for the right reasons and one of the ways to do that is by always saying 'Yes'.

Or we get trapped into just saying 'Yes' to everything because it's habit or because it's easier (saying 'No' really is a skill they should teach from Nursery- they must have started this since I left school as my own kids say it regularly). This has to be one of the hardest habits to break!

Don't get me wrong! Ambition- great! Dedication- superb! Commitment- yes indeed! Helping out- yes please! Volunteering- great idea!

The thing that we need to consider is that in reality we are all going to be teaching / leading for longer before we retire and the job (while being the best job in the Universe- and I truly mean that) is getting harder! We can't keep doing everything under the sun! Especially when other people should be doing things that we find ourselves doing just because we're asked! But we still do!

The idea is all about balance! If you get the balance right you will be more effective in what it is that you do! Carefully select what you volunteer for! But by no means stop volunteering! Just take a few moments careful consideration before that 3 letter word escapes and you're in a situation you might regret later when you don't have time to do what you needed to do before midnight arrives and you have to go to bed!

As school leaders it is essential that we create an environment where it is Ok to say 'No' at every level but only when it is appropriate! A fine balance indeed! By doing this you will create a more effective staff who are able to do their jobs to the best of their abilities.

As school leaders we have to learn to say 'No' too! How often do we find ourselves offering to call so and so because someone asked us to but it's their responsibility and their non-contact time? I've always said 'Yes' so the answer is obvious and instinctive! Sometimes it's easier! Sometimes it's quicker! Sometimes I don't even realise I've said it until the task is my responsibility- it's a habit!

We always left school late as NQT's so why wouldn't we leave even later, as leaders, every single night? It's habit after all and our 'To Do' lists are longer and the reality is that we need to do more! But how often do we leave late because we were doing something someone else could and should have done! Why is our evening meal dry, shrivelled and crispy? Because we said 'Yes' when we shouldn't have!

By saying 'No' when it's appropriate or thinking about our response before it jumps out of our mouths we might just get home that little bit sooner some nights which would be nice! And the food we eat may even taste like it should!

Sometimes things do need doing! Other times they need doing but not by you!

Saying 'No' is difficult when you are used to saying 'Yes' all of the time and it's something we need to remind ourselves of. Saying that I still find myself saying 'Yes' on a regular basis and that isn't such a bad thing too....

Like a healthy diet or lifestyle coach would say- 'BALANCE'!

BIG Mistake No 27: Giving Up Too Soon

Don Smith
Speaker & Trainer

When you find yourself at the end of your;
tether, energy, wits, whatever, at that moment,
when you just want to give up and run, at that
moment ...

This is what you do...

When you are in that terrible place and the
illusion of fear seems too bright to bear and the
false apprehension of disaster is twisting at you
inside.

This is what you do...

Keep breathing! Keep breathing!

Keep looking and listening!

Deal with things as they really are... not with how bad they could be!

Never stop yourself... let the situation or the problem stop you... it rarely will!

Know that there absolutely is a solution... probably more than one...

Some of them really easy... keep seeking for it/them!

When you get over/past/through it... as you almost certainly will..

You will be stronger, wiser and more able than before!

When you get over/past/through it...

remember these words...

for the next time...

and in the meantime...

share them!

BIG Mistake No 28:
Letting them forget you

Paul Ronayne

40 years on and I still clearly remember my favourite teacher. I have never forgotten him because his appearance, demeanour and simple connectivity with his student's engendered a respect, esteem and deference that was as enduring as crystal. In effect he became a role model for me.

Your students WILL remember you, long after you have forgotten them but will it be for the right reasons? In the wake of recent serious civil disorder in England many politicians, educationalists and sociologists have been calling for better role models for young people but do they really know what a role-model is? Ask your pupils who their role models are and take note of their answers; what they believe a role model is and why.

In amongst the celebrities and football stars there may be the occasional historical character or close relative. Build on these and ask why they would like to emulate such people and why they consider them appropriate role models. Try to stress that fame and fortune are not necessary requirements and combine your views with your natural optimism, confidence and most of all respect for the answers you receive from your students.

We live in the global world of mega-communication that bombards us constantly with the benefits of a celebrity, fame and fortune society. It should not be any surprise to anyone that young people are influenced by this culture and want to subscribe into it.

As teachers and educationalists we are placed in a unique position to influence our students for the greater good. Work towards this goal and maybe one day they will be able to tell their family, friends and colleagues that they have a role model, one they won't forget.

BIG Mistake No 29: Believing the myth that the teacher rules

Donna Feldman, Ph.D.
English Teacher - Cleveland Heights High School
Literacy Consultant and Speaker

In a way, a classroom is like a small kingdom with the teacher holding the monarchy and the students the vassals. The teacher creates the system of laws, rewards and punishments, and taxes. The student is there to learn and obey while the teacher rules from her throne.

Wrong.

Governments without representation have rebellions.
Classrooms without relationships have behaviour problems.
While the teacher is the adult responsible for all aspects of the classroom, the better scenario for a classroom is a democracy in which the ruling

body listens and responds to the masses by foraging relationships with students. Students today, especially those in low-income areas, have experiences beyond our imagination. Many may not have an adult in their lives with whom they can discuss problem or goals. The frustration they feel translates to disorder in your class.

Relationships entail conversation. Greet each student at the door as they enter your room. This time is also a good opportunity to compliment them. Commenting that a girl's new shirt is pretty or a boy's shoes are sharp makes students know you are aware of them. The door conversation is also wonderful way to compliment the work they do in your class. Another good time to provide compliments is when you circulate the room during times your students are working independently or in small groups.

Good relationships are enhanced with respect. What better way to show respect than with manners. By adding the words please, thank you, and you're welcome when you make requests of students you will see the feel of your class changes from bossy to friendly.

Remember – you catch more bees with honey than vinegar. By making your students feel important and emotionally good in your class, you create a kingdom of caring. Becoming a kind benevolent ruler rather than a tyrant will result in the climate you want for your classroom.

BIG Mistake No 30: Ignoring the Signs of the Red Zone

Donna Feldman

You've heard the expression, "seeing red", and as a teacher, you'll see it firsthand time and time again. When a student sees red, he is angry, and ignoring his anger may prove to be disruptive to your class. Anger is not difficult to detect but does require an attentive eye. The physical signs of anger include a flushed face with a frown, eyes in a fixed hard stare, the nose flared out, the lips drawn back, a clenched jaw, eyebrows positioned inward and downward, and a voice that is higher than normal. While you're seeing this, the student is feeling physically warm, tense, impulsive, and ready to explode with the need to strike out at something or somebody.

Few if any of your education classes prepared you for confronting a student this angry. You may feel inadequate to handle the student. Rather than let the anger escalate and explode in your classroom, there are some easy cool-downs you can have the student do.

IGNORING THE SITUATION WILL NOT MAKE IT GO AWAY.

Students become angry over the loss of a cell phone, argument with a friend or family member or another teacher, bad grade, or just a bad hair day.
Acknowledge the student's anger with an "I statement"; I see you look angry. Ask the angry student to remove any outwear so he can cool down physically. Suggest to the student, he take a few deep and relaxing breaths.
If you have a good relationship with the student prior to this situation, he may disclose the source of his anger to you. If possible, have the other students begin their assignment while you discuss the situation with the student in a corner or in the hallway. If a conversation is not possible, suggest the student write about why he is angry.

Once you have the source of the student's angry, you can determine the best way to proceed. Is the angry recurring and symptomatic of a larger problem? Does the student need to see a counsellor or other student support staff member? Does security or an administrator need to become involved? Do you contact the parents/guardian?

Have a plan in place for defusing your angry students on the first day of school. Check your school policy. You'll feel better when you're prepared and so will your students.

BIG Mistake No 31: Not smiling until Christmas

James Waite
Head of a special school for pupils with severe behavioural difficulties

I am told that some NQTs are still being advised during teacher training that on taking up their first appointment "not to smile until Christmas" – the basis being that showing any form of positive emotion must be a sign of weakness that children will exploit.

As an NQT I was in the strange position of also being a very young Head of Year which involved overseeing the behaviour of 250 children in an inner-city comprehensive. A senior colleague's advice was to 1) find a child talking in my first assembly, make them stand up and shout at them (to scare pupils into behaving appropriately) and 2) stand over and bawl at the worst behaved pupils across the school in public (eg. on a corridor in front of others to exemplify how big, tough and loud I could be).

Some years later and I now work solely with the 'worst behaved' children in special schools where shouting is banned, calmness is key and positive relationships drawing upon professionals' emotional intelligence, empathy and communication skills are at the centre of our success with pupils.

Take an example of many a boy I've worked with – Nathan, 13. It's Monday morning, an English lesson and I politely ask Nathan to take his seat and remove his cap, which he does in his own slow way whilst quietly muttering 'f*ck off, man'. As an NQT, I can shamefully say that I hit the roof, screamed something along the lines of "how dare you speak to me like that; get of my classroom!" and subsequently followed him out to continue my rant at his appalling attitude. Nathan ends up in tears and runs away. In other situations the same ridiculous reaction from the adult can result in a shouting match or an assault on the teacher – usually resulting in a fixed-term exclusion for the pupil.

What I do now is think before I speak. Has Nathan had a horrendous weekend? Is he shouted at in his home? Is he wanting attention and therefore by reacting I'm giving him what he wants? As a pupil I know well, is this out of character for him? Or is he just a rude teenager getting away with telling his parents to do the same thing?

Nathan is actually doing what I've asked and by the time his seat is taken and his cap's off, I verbally ignore the comment but my eye contact with him ensures he and others know I've heard what he said. Once he's sat, ready to learn, I thank him. I teach the lesson.

As I dismiss pupils at the end of the lesson, I ask Nathan to stay behind. I know him and have taken time to understand how he calms down, thinks things through and processes information.
I have a civil conversation with him, using open-ended questions to facilitate his agreement that if I told him to 'f*ck off' on a Monday morning he probably 'wouldn't like it, sir'.

The result is 1) no drama has resulted, 2) no learning has been unnecessarily interrupted and 3) Nathan knows that his use of offensive language was disrespectful and unacceptable.

There's also a consequence because Nathan will spend half of his lunchtime with me in detention. Plus, even though I haven't stressed myself out shouting and making a show of a situation, the other pupils can see I've picked up on Nathan's remark and taken action.

Clear rules, boundaries and consistent application of rewards and sanctions are, of course, crucial in the classroom but the best teachers foster positive relationships, use body language, eye contact and praise to keep classrooms calm, happy and enjoyable places to be.

It's not a crime to joke with, smile and be pleasant to children and certainly won't make you a weak teacher. Listening to children, making the effort to know and understand them and then using this knowledge to develop rewarding relationships feels so much better than days spent shouting and frowning.

Feel free to build relationships well before Christmas.

BIG Mistake No 32: Not absolutely, definitely, positively, knowing your stuff

Jane Pallister
MD of Boommm Consultancy and Training
Part time lecturer
Business mentor and trainer for Staffordshire and Keele Universities.

There's no excuse for not absolutely, definitely, positively knowing your stuff when you teach or present.

I have seen so many people cling to PowerPoint slides slavishly, not moving away from the text and being unable to expand and bring in anecdotal information, or engage with the audience by asking questions about their experiences and allowing their input to feed back into your subject.

People don't want you to fail when you speak, but they have been marketed to and/or opted for your course and, understandably, there is an expectation that you will be knowledgeable and add value.

It's critical to remember, it's not about you - it's about the audience. It's about delivering benefits. Moving people forward. Adding to their knowledge and skill-set. Capturing attention and creating motivation.

It does not matter how big the audience is or what type of presentation you are making. It doesn't matter whether it's a light subject or something heavy. You could be pitching to one client, or speaking to the masses. It's your job to do your homework: assess the audience needs and wants, and meet these by absolutely knowing your stuff.

What you should focus on is giving your audience new information that meets three primary requirements – to be valuable, usable and memorable.

If you know your subject inside out and always deliver on these primary requirements, your audience will respect you and remember you.

BIG Mistake No 33: Labelling students

Jason Menzinger MIfL

Some teachers are quick to label students either in a negative or positive light, the class clown, the good and the bad.

Labels are all formed from opinions and experiences and not always in a professional context.

Did you know Jimmy refused to read out loud in class because he has dyslexia or Linda gets angry and walks out of class because when you raise your voice at her it triggers behaviour she has to deal with from her abusive drunk father?

As professionals our duty of care goes as far as reading your student file and having a complete understanding of each individual. Planning and preparing lessons in context with those individuals is exactly what teaching is all about and by having a professional approach those labels can be generally ironed out or catered for.

I strongly recommend taking time out and making time for students and using strategies such as motivational dialogue to build lasting relationships. It is all too very easy to start labelling students but please have an open mind and do not fall in the trap of gossiping in the staff room.

Students love personal targets and a bad apple on their own can always be turned round with strategies that will get them thinking.

Make your own professional judgement and read the learners profiles.

BIG Mistake No 34: Don't underestimate the power of YOU!

Andy Cope
Author, trainer and learning junkie
http://www.artofbrilliance.co.uk

Kung Fu Panda...epic story of martial arts, ancient mystical powers, enlightenment and, err, noodle soup?

Our hero is a rather rotund and accident-prone panda. Panda's dad (a bird who owns and runs a noodle outlet... don't ask!) tells him that he feels Panda is ready to take over the running of the shop and that one day he will tell him the way to make his 'Special Ingredient' noodle soup.

But the Panda is destined for greater things – he travels across China to take on the mantle of the Dragon Warrior, facing pain, tiredness and stamina-sapping physical and mental tests until he is ready to receive the Dragon Scroll. The

Scroll is an ancient parchment that is reserved only for viewing by the true Dragon Warrior. He will need its secrets to fight the mighty challenger to his new title.

To his horror he finds that he cannot read the scroll, there is no writing upon it; no writing means no secret – he must fight the challenger on his own!

Yikes!

Full of self-doubt, he meets up again with his dad who announces, with some gravity, that he has something to tell his son. Panda listens, hoping to find out how he can be a Panda when his father is a Crane! Instead, his father offers this jaw-dropper, 'Son, there is no special ingredient in the 'Special Ingredient' Noodle Soup. It's just that people believe there is.'

 No way!

Equally there is no special secret in the scroll, it is made of reflective paper and reveals, when you look at it, that 'you' are the special ingredient!
(There's a message in there somewhere folks!)

BIG Mistake No 35: Not using the microphone (it won't bite!)

Lee Jackson
Education speaker and Author
www.leejackson.org

Speaking up front is good for you.

Can you think of a major leader over the last century who wasn't a good speaker? Presentation skills are a key to your success. Harvard Business School's research discovered that people who present well get to the top of the tree.

I have worked in schools for many years and also deliver speaking skills training to senior staff. One of the reasons I do this training is that there is a massive need for it!

Over the years I have seen loads of teachers and even high level education "experts" refuse to use the microphone in assemblies, staff training days and conferences. It's almost an allergy in the public sector.

Once, I even saw a member of SLT walk up to the microphone at the front of the presentation evening and then take three side steps to the right of the mic - avoiding it completely, then doing a talk that no-one could hear.

Honestly you couldn't make this stuff up. It didn't help their reputation or the schools, it was a little embarrassing.

Every teacher knows how to speak to 32 students in a classroom, but once you have to speak to a larger group a new set of skills is needed.

Here's a few tips to help:

1. Practice doesn't make perfect but it's essential for success.

Take the chance to do assemblies etc and just give it a go. There are loads of resources out there to help, and also get a friend to give you feedback afterwards. Learn from it and do it again and again. The more you do it the better you'll get.

2. "Catch on fire with enthusiasm and people will come for miles to watch you burn." John Wesley.

Speak about something you know and are passionate about, don't ever "speak to someone else's slides" or about a subject you know little about. Young people can see that very clearly, i sometimes say no to paid work because someone else could do it better than me. I speak on what i know.

3. "Be yourself, everyone else is taken" - Oscar Wilde.

Finding your natural style is really important, but remember to be appropriate too. I've seen all sorts of cringe-worthy moments over the years and even saw an inappropriate assembly that contributed significantly to the sacking of a head teacher!

4. "A joke is a very serious thing" Winston Churchill.

Be amusing, but don't tell jokes, they divide the

audience. Also don't put down other staff, subjects or students, keep it positive, thats always the best option.

5. Check out your venue before you speak and do a little rehearsal.

A lot of anxiety about speaking is the fear of the unknown, so by checking out the venue and technical stuff beforehand you will reduce your nerves and do much better. I arrive at a venue at least 30-60 minutes before I speak, that can make the difference between a good and bad talk.

Have fun!

BIG Mistake No 36: Scrimping on Marking

Lucy Metcalfe
Head of Media Studies
Writer and Presenter of Media CPD

Teachers often moan about marking; how it adds to their workload, thinking it's a futile way of spending hours with a red pen in hand for little result. However, marking can be a key way of making contact with your students, of telling them you're listening to them and helping them make real progress.

Imagine, you have spent an hour of your free time working on a piece of work. It isn't returned to you for several weeks, and then when you do lay eyes on it, it simply says 'good work'. This is not the way to inspire young minds!

Marking is well worth the time spent if you make it quality feedback. That doesn't mean you need to spend hours and hours over the books, but for each piece of work you set, where students are expected to produce an individual response, it's a good idea to give them the courtesy of individual feedback.

Try writing a positive comment first of all. For example, 'What an interesting story', or 'A well-written analysis of...'. Then think of a couple of ways the piece of work could be improved. Could the student develop their line of argument further? Perhaps, they need to reference more accurately? It could be a simple improvement technique like, 'Structure your work into clear paragraphs – new topic, new time, new location = new paragraph'.
For students who excel in your subject, it's sometimes tricky to think of targets in this way. So why not ask them a question to stretch their thinking? You could set them a challenge to find out something else about the topic, or get them to read an article which is linked. Just don't leave it at 'good work'. How can this inspire further learning?

One of the biggest mistakes with marking is to spend the hours plodding through the books and then do nothing with this. Marking is a conversation with your students. If you were talking with them, wouldn't you want them to say something back? So, make sure after each marking exercise, the students respond in some way. They could write a reply to your comment. For example, 'Fair point Sir, I will work on adding examples to illustrate my points next time.' Better still; get them to redraft part of the work to show, not only that have they listened, but also that they can do what you're suggesting. You could also get your students to highlight or circle where they have made changes, or where they are going to develop in their next piece. This way you can see where they are making progress and the marking will seem so much more worthwhile.

Make your marking mean something. It's a great way of showing your students you care about them and their work and you'll be surprised at how well they respond to the feedback in their progress and enthusiasm for their work.

BIG Mistake No 37: Leaving out the Context

Lucy Metcalfe
Head of Media Studies
Writer and Presenter of Media CPD

If you don't make your lessons 'real' it's little wonder students will leave them thinking 'what's the point'? Imagine you have to study some complex maths concepts for example. If they are just numbers on the page, it's going to be hard to see why you have to solve them, other than to make your teacher happy. Or perhaps you have to write a review of a book you've read in class. If this is simply to finish the topic, it does seem to be a rather dull exercise.

However, even the most dreary topics and theories must fit somewhere in the real world. If you can make this happen in your classroom, your students will not only develop their understanding more easily, but will find the lessons much more engaging.

Take the examples above again. Wouldn't it be a lot easier to deal with the maths if the problems were related to the real world? They could be linked, for example, to running a business eg working out floor space at an exhibition, how much stock you would need to sell at what price to create a profit. This seems like a much more realistic challenge and sets students up with, not just the skills for your lesson, but with life skills too. If the English book review was linked to a national book prize and the students were the judges, this might get them more motivated to really think about their review writing techniques. Perhaps the review could be translated into a televised critics' show with some help from your Media department. Again, this creates a real purpose for the writing and a great end product for students to be truly proud of.

In many subjects, it may well be possible to invent role play scenarios to engage the students with the topic material. In studying music promotion, either in Media or Music itself, could you get students to play the roles of A&R scouts, researchers, song writers, tour managers, choreographers, vocal coaches or designers? They scenario could involve some great group work activities, with an end goal of getting your artist to reach number one. Through working in this kind of environment, students are also developing skills they may use in their careers later on. They might not work in the music industry, but isn't it possible that they'll have to work in a team, come up with creative ideas and present a pitch to their bosses one day?

Whatever your subject, if you can draw the work back to where it's used in the real world, you'll nearly always find tricky topics become much more manageable for your classes and potentially uninspiring content will be transformed by the creative young minds that you have switched on.

BIG Mistake No 38:
Thinking others decide
how we will live our lives

Lynn Grocott
Speaker , Trainer & Confidence Coach

What if: "I Decide"

Are your students really aware of their true inner resources?

What if you could wake up their "passion" for life?

Let me show you how this worked for me... going from a woman walking on two sticks due to the nature of multiple sclerosis, allowing the baggage of life, including the suicide of both parents, bullying and much more, to give me the excuse of living the victim...

I found my purpose.

A mother and baby unit had to be built in Cameroon and eleven thousand pounds had to be raised. Using the phrase "What if I can" the money to build the unit was raised and the unit is now up and running. My book was written and published and the success grew and grew in other areas of my life, turning victim to victor.

So what if you enable your students to discover what works for them? Ask searching questions, enable them to find real passion and desire,

What if you show them to turn the phrase "what if?" from negative to positive, for instance "What if this is easier than I think", "What if I can find someone to support me?"

What if you can enable them to turn their lives from woe to wow!

How good will it make you feel?!

BIG Mistake No 39: Not having Venues for Emotional Expression

Donna Feldman, Ph.D.
English Teacher - Cleveland Heights High School
Literacy Consultant and Speaker

With the requirements of testing, writing can now be found in almost all classrooms. Writing assignments are commonly given to literature, history, math processes, and science reports. The completion rate of writing assignment varies on genre and subject.

We all know that.

Writing is, however, overlooked in the discussion of classroom management. Its uses for improved student behaviour are as numerous as those of academic subjects.

Writing a paragraph or two about inappropriate

behavior provides an unobtrusive opportunity for students to reflect on the behavior that prompted the poor behaviour in the first place. Students can use writing to examine the trigger to their behaviour and brainstorm ways to avoid the situation in the future.

Upon hearing inappropriate language, one teacher had her offenders identify a substitute word and write why that word would be better to use than profanity.

I use writing to defuse tempers and investigate offenses that occurred both in and out of my class. This genre can be passed on to administrators and security for preventative measures. Venting on paper is far less distracting than venting with speech!

Writing provides privacy when disclosing adversity. By expelling the trauma or negative feelings the student has, he will become less frustrated, less disruptive, and more productive.

Writing is said to be thinking. Students can write their opinions about current topics. They can write warm, fuzzy compliments to their classmates, identifying the strengths of their colleagues. The words on paper serve as an affirmation of their beliefs and will guide their actions.

By using writing to defuse anger, vent frustration, and find the good in situations and people, you will make it more difficult for students to misbehave and improve their writing skills at the same time!

BIG Mistake No 40: No One Leaves My Room!

Donna Feldman, Ph.D.
English Teacher - Cleveland Heights High School
Literacy Consultant and Speaker

To everything there is a season. A time to learn and a time to teach. A time to cooperate and a time to disagree. A time to behave and a time to disrupt.
Just ask your students. They will find time for EVERYTHING in your class including activities that you do not want such sketching, passing notes, sleeping, talking to a friend, texting, talking on their cell phones, arguing with you, quarrelling with another student, and being a severe behaviour problem.

For severe behaviour, it's okay to send students out of your room.
Repeat the above sentence until you (1) believe it, and (2) are willing to do it.
There is a time to keep students in class and a time to remove them.

Your job is to know how to decide.

One mantra for helping you to decide is – the punishment must fit the crime.
If a student is sketching, is it because she finished her work? Is the note passed a request for help, either for an academic issue or a social problem? Is the student sleeping because he lives with an infant, has a job after school, or took a parent to the hospital? If you have a relationship with your students, you will know the answers to these questions.

The correct response to these behaviour issues is one of clarification or mild rebuke.

When a student talks to another at an inappropriate time, investigate the cause. All too often, one student will help another during your lesson. If the talking is not about anything relevant to school and continues, more dire actions are needed. The students can be separated. If that fails, I send the chief culprit for a short time out. The removal from a inappropriate situation provides an opportunity for the student to regroup and rethink his behavior.
Short time outs often defuse a volatile situation between two students. Should the pattern

reoccur between them, peer mediation or conflict resolution may in order and take place outside your class.

Repeated arguing with you can be dangerous and undermine your classroom goals. If it becomes disruptive, the student involved needs to go.
Surprisingly, most of our students prefer to be in the class rather than removed. But, as the person responsible for the safety and well-being of all you students, you make the decision on removal. Check school policy to make sure you make the right decision.

BIG Mistake No 41: Leaving for tomorrow what you should have done today

Nigel Vardy
Motivational Speaker & Author
http://www.nigelvardy.com

It's the same old story - I'll do my homework or lesson plans on Sunday evening rather than Friday night.

What does this do?

Well, you dwell all weekend on what's coming up Sunday and then do your work poorly. Why not do it straight away on Friday, get it out of the way and then have a great weekend..?

Modern society seems caught up in a world of laise faire attitudes. Action needs to be taken!

As a Mountaineer I have learned that work and

jobs that need doing immediately, should be. Time (and in my case) the weather wait for no-one and if I haven't correctly built the tent/ stored gear/got cooking on time then anything can (and does) happen!

Planning an expedition takes critical time management and every minute counts.

I cannot afford to lose my concentration on a mountain or it could cost me my life! You can't afford to lose concentration on your teaching or education. This is your future and you need to take action!

These may be extreme examples, but the same lesson goes thorough life. Get done what needs to be done, get it out of the ways and get on with your life. Dwelling on the matter won't cure it - it will just make it worse..!

BIG Mistake No 42: Forgetting to tie your clothes line securely

Jeremy Renals
Maths Coach & Speaker

If you're keeping a speech together in front of an audience, forgetting to "Clothes Line" is a sure-fire recipe for messy delivery and disengaged punters.

"Clothes Lining" is a simple technique to make a presentation more effective, making up for the elements you can't plan exactly. It works on the basis that first impressions last, and last impressions last.

Imagine a clothes line. You tie one end securely. Then you tie the other end securely. Presto! The middle takes care of itself naturally. This principle can be applied to public speaking, or many other instances where you need to think on your feet: get the beginning pinned down perfectly, plan an effective end right down to the exact few words, and the middle can be managed with a relatively rough plan of what you should be doing.

It's a mistake to attempt to plan every word of a speech, even one as short as two minutes. You'll waste valuable effort memorising each word, for example a written script, and then if you come off the rails you'll flounder trying to remember the precise words you were looking for at that point.

Far better if you know what you're talking about just to say it. For sure you'll need to plan some broad brush strokes, but if you know your stuff you can plan what to talk about and then just say it. The result is more natural, flexible, and economical on effort.

However, learning an exact opening sentence is an effort well worth making, as it will set you on your way with confidence; a springboard if you like. Similarly, a precisely practised closing phrase will be something to pull yourself towards at the end, and will leave your audience with an impression of certainty and confidence. Delivered well it will guarantee applause.

So beware. Neglect to clothes line, and your

entry may be a confusion that you never recover from, and your exit may be a blur that's unsatisfactory for everyone.

Big Mistake No 43: You need to be 'born with natural talent'

Penny Mallory
Speaker

There is no such thing as being 'born with natural talent'

No one is born with a natural talent, or a special gift. I am convinced we are all born 'a clean sheet of paper' and our lives will be influenced by family, friends, teachers, environments and experiences.

What do you think the word 'talent' actually means? Is it a word to describe a seemingly outstanding ability - one that sets someone apart from the masses? I will have to assume you agree that's a pretty acceptable definition of the word talent.

Now I want to challenge this, and ask you to reconsider for a moment. It will be worth it, I promise.

I was not 'born to drive rally cars' or 'born with a talent to drive'; instead I went to a rally school and learnt how to do it. The more lessons I had, the better I got. With ten years of practice and experience, I was able to compete at World Championship level. And what a ball I had, but that's not my point.

Tiger Woods was born no more talented at golf than you or I. But he was born to parents who taught him to swing a club and hit a ball, from the age of 1. He practiced, rehearsed and trained until he became the one of the most successful golfers of all time. Tiger worked hard on his put, driving, concentration, mental imagery and every conceivable aspect of his game. He simply worked harder than anyone else. The more work he put in, the better he got. As another golfing legend, Jack Nicklaus, pointed out, 'The more I practice, the luckier I get'.

So called 'child prodigies' are no more than children who have studied hard and practiced more than their contemporaries. Mozart had been composing music since the age of 3, so it was hardly surprising that he was writing mind blowing world class symphonies in his teens.

David Beckham became a world class footballer because he worked harder than anyone on his ball skills. Eight year olds that multiply 13 digits numbers together have been working with numbers and maths from the age of 18 months.

Practice, rehearsal and repetition makes you outstanding. You are not born brilliant - you become brilliant through hard work!

Oh and it's worth remembering that Einstein's brain was made exactly the same as yours, it's just that he used his better, and worked it harder.

So, all those students in your class have amazing abilities and incredible potential. If they work hard they will do well. With a passion to learn, becoming World Class is down to about 10,000 hours or ten years of practice.

There is no such thing as talent. Ask Tiger.

Big Mistake No 44: Not smiling

Hannah Yaawusuah Adjepong
Inspire & Bless Ltd.
www.inspireandbless.co.uk

SMILE!

As we walk daily through crowded streets or
quiet lanes,
we pass by people from all walks of life.
There may be some whose hearts are burdened
with sorrow, disappointment and stress.
Do we fully understand what a smile could
bring to the people we meet?
Have we any idea what life may have thrown at
those who may
appear unfriendly to us?
Yet a smile could be like sunshine and kind
words may lift the gloom.
We may never know what we communicate
many a time

even without words.
Each day brings its own shadows into our lives
but we know
there must be sunshine out there to create the
shadows.
The truth remains however that sunshine and
shadows
though opposites need not be enemies.
We can beam rays of light into other people's
lives
when we appreciate in our own the uplifting a
smile brings.
Smile today at the people you meet, someone
will be blessed by it.
You may bring sunshine in someone's life
simply by smiling.
And even if no one reciprocates your kindness
rest assured that a smile like sunshine is never
wasted.

Big Mistake No 45: Being an island

Neil Glasspool
Vice Principal

Once the general Induction sessions are over staff continue to be developed but obviously spend most of their time in their departments and, if lucky, their own room. Teaching is a busy job – loads to do. Lots of deadlines, things to remember and people checking this and that are done on time. Then, of course all the planning, marking and preparation time. Oh, and a life outside of teaching too!!!

With all this in mind it is so easy just to keep yourself to yourself, see who you need to see and just try to do the best job you can. But, you have maybe over a hundred other adults working with you, all trying to do a good job, but all who have something to offer you and usually are more than willing to give you a few minutes and maybe so much more.

The buddy – someone who you can just share a

kind word with to have a smile during the day.
The shoulder – someone who is great at
listening and can sympathise with you over
issues you are finding stressful.
The sage – someone (not necessarily older) who
has been through what you are going through
and can offer quick, simple solutions.
The tipster – someone who is just full of good
ideas, tips, etc.
The expert –someone who knows about ICT,
good twitter sites, where to find stuff, who to
speak to and who to avoid!

Then there are all the members of staff who can
give you advice over a particular class or
student who you may be struggling with – most
students will have at least 8 other teachers. Ask
to observe them! All these people have lives too!

Someone may have the same interest as you.
Perhaps they also play your favourite sport /
hobby and can advise on a local club to join. Or
just to have a chat about that TV programme
that no-one else watches.

Someone who has your sense of humour and
you may never talk "shop" to but makes you
laugh.

Fed up with lugging your books in your trendy Sainsbury's bag-for-life on the bus – someone is bound to live close to you and can offer a lift either regularly (saves them money if share petrol!) or after Parents' Evenings.

Future life partner ......

Once you get chatting, then you may surprise yourself how much you have to offer others too!

Big Mistake No 46: Taking notice of negative perceptions expressed by other teachers

Tony Burgess
Coach and Trainer
http:// www.aha-success.com

Staff rooms are often places where teachers compare notes and share perceptions with colleagues about classes and individual students. Sometimes perceptions expressed are constructive and at the other extreme can be outright negative.

I do understand that voicing negatives can be a way for a teacher to 'get something off their chest' and at the same time there is an inbuilt danger with the sharing of such views.

I remember when I first arrived in post to teach at a school and I was interacting with other teachers in the staff room as I settled into the new workplace.

Before I had even met my classes or got to know specific students, I was offered many comments such as "You'll have to watch out for _____ – he is trouble!" and "_____ is really disruptive, she'll give you the run-around" and "Good luck with class ___ - You're going to need it" and other similar comments. There were of course many positive comments offered about students and classes too.

I know that these messages were offered with positive intention for me; to prepare me and forewarn me. The problem though was that I'd now got some preconceived ideas about students and classes that I had not even met – ideas that, to a degree, had me 'expecting' trouble and had my mind 'primed' for noticing problems.

The danger here is that people tend to get more of what they look for and expect and this can prompt a kind of self-fulfilling prophecy. When a teacher goes into a classroom with a preconceived idea that 'this group is trouble' then they are going to be in a different state to if they were more open-minded or expecting the best.

This unconsciously affects body-language, tonality and approach of the teacher that will signal to the class what the teacher believes about them. And this indirectly invites responses from students that are consistent with the teacher's beliefs and expectations. This in turn ends up 'proving' the teacher's perceptions to have been 'true' and perpetuates the message that 'this class is trouble'.

Being a psychology specialist, I knew the dangers of adopting preconceived ideas (about anything) and so to an extent was ready to resist fully accepting the negative perceptions offered by other teachers and instead make the decision to find out for myself. Having said that, the seed of an idea had been sown and it was hard work for me to completely dismiss the views that had delivered to me so convincingly.

Just as I would warn you against taking on other teachers' negative perceptions, I would also warn you against offering such negative perceptions to colleagues yourself.

If you feel that a colleague needs forewarning about a class or a student, first of all remember that the experiences you have had are your experiences and that it is far from inevitable that the same will be experienced by your colleague. Secondly, make your comments as positive as possible.

"This class shows a wide range of behaviours and you may need to keep flexible to get the best out of these students" would be enough to flag up that they may need to be particularly resourceful.

Big Mistake No 47: Not taking charge of what you do

Gary Chalmers
Very Experienced Physics Teacher and Educational Leader

Vary what you do and take educational risks. Pupils have 5-8 lessons per day (depending on the school); if they are all the same, the most able pupils switch off. Doing things differently keeps pupils on their toes (and keeps you interested). Enjoying variety is a sign of potential to be a successful individual. I once spoke to a pupil who said that she went up the hill to school with a full pen and down the hill with an empty pen.

Strategies work some of the time and come and go - creating a learning culture works every time! Establish what you want your pupils to be like and make that a consistent expectation (as long as you do not contradict the previous rule). Aim to establish your culture for 95% of your pupils - the other 5% will follow!

Manage your time - put all administrative tasks in your planner, including marking and responding to emails etc... When your schedule is disrupted, make a note of it also. When planning these tasks, allow plenty of time for them: having a little bit of time left over is very useful for ensuring that the work is finished off and that you have contacted form tutors etc. about any work that is either a cause for concern or delight!

Make a niche for yourself with after school activities. That way you get to have more fun (in many cases you get to indulge in your hobbies for free) as well and are less likely to get roped into supervising activities which do not interest you.

Big Mistake No 48: Ignoring the art of backwards

Carl Barton
Lecturer

I suppose you could say I am an accidental academic; teaching was never really a plan for me until I found myself travelling the country speaking to bigger and bigger groups.

From High School to Universities via Prisoners and students with specialist requirements, I found that one skill I used always out performs any other.
I call it the art of backwards. Any student taking any course has a desired outcome for their attendance. Our job is to covertly install the learning outcomes of the topic into the student without them noticing we have done this, if successful this installs a desire for further knowledge.

But inevitably some students do not engage

with courses and that too is ok as long as they are not disruptive and are encouraged to find the right path for them. I have my own formula (it works for me, so I am not saying it's a magic bullet).

I introduce myself, and at the start of the year try to remember as many names as possible. I try to remember something unique about them (band t-shirt, favourite sport, who they like / hate).

In the first tutorial I ask them why they want the skills from this module, what is their dream job again them not knowing is also ok. We listen not force.   This is like placing a microchip on a computer.
I perhaps make a note on the digital register if I feel they will need more attention a * will do.

My own learning is helped by getting the students to sign the first register, I can normally tell a student's confidence / ego by the signature. I install the students in my memory. Here's an example.

John puts a hand up (he is wearing a heavy metal shirt and loves drumming). I will answer the question (hopefully). And programme that virtual microchip by finishing my answer with something like " you got that..... rock on" in a NATURAL VOICE.

Then if I hit a problem with a student's motivation and they give me a list of complaints and frustration. I can work backwards to switch the virtual microchip on like a sat nav with the destination programmed to the learning outcome.

So a few weeks later, and John has major frustration with an aspect of the course. He calls me over.

1.   Smile

2.   Get him to state the problem

3.   Ask him what he has tried

4.   Try to bridge the gap answer the question in my own mind

5.   If it's out of his control fix it and explain what was wrong (example software settings changed and not returned to previous settings by student on higher level)

6.   If he is happy to try again, give him an

agreed time and return to check on progress

7.   If he is frustrated and says "I HATE /
THIS DONT GET THIS" reach in the toolbox
and remind him of his dream / hero and re-
ignite the goal or use the example to show how
they could learn this like their hero. "This is a
fundamental part of your dream it's like a
drummer turning up for the gig with no
drumsticks"

8.   Don't be scared of challenging them
using something they hate. "So your
SERIOUSLY telling me you can be beaten by
this. I bet if you were being paid you would find
a way....... (WAIT FOR THE YES) because ?????
as soon as they try to speak cut across them with
(ITS A JOB AND SO THIS.....) I would employ
you, because I know you can do it..... but let me
ask you a question " WOULD YOU EMPLOY
YOU WITH THIS ATTITUDE"..... (Wait for the
NO). You got this....." I then asses if I can leave
them and call back or go back to stage 3

9.   Congratulate the room on their work for
the day and preview next week, finishing with
the deadline.... "Nice one for today, we are
getting there. Next week we transfer the film to
DVD. We have a lot to do so be on time and

think about what's left to do... see me now if there are any issues"

10.   Stop John on the way out apologise for being abrupt, but the biggest frustration for teachers is talented people wasting that talent (no matter what level he is actually at)

CONGRATULATIONS YOU HAVE JUST SWITCHED ON HIS SATNAV !

Big Mistake No 49: Restraining the Force

Nina Smith

Let's face it: there is an enormous power and capacity for learning hidden inside each and every student. We just cannot find it, and thus make it work against us.

We all are born with the need to understand and tools to experience life and make sense of what we see, hear and feel. And we use the information we gather from our everyday lives to construct our understanding about ourselves, the life, universe and everything – AND about the things we learn at school. This is the driving force behind all real learning.

So, here is the task for us as educators: how to tap into that force, and make it work for us instead of against us?

Depending on the feedback students receive about their explorations they will either continue to the direction they are headed, or venture into something else. And exactly here lies our biggest mistake. Instead of unleashing that force at schools, we tend to restrain it. Why??

Is it only because we desire to have control over the small details of what students learn? Or choose the way how learning happens? Or is it because we think we have been told we should control these things?

Being able to go with the flow of learning force makes teaching and learning easy and enjoyable. Providing timely and accurate feedback convinces students that they are on the right track and therefore they are driven to find out more. This is also the basic recipe for strengthening intrinsic motivation.
Providing different options for learning tasks takes the culmination point away from the power struggle (you must do this because I say so), and allows students follow their own passion and also learn how to choose wisely (this is equally true with High School students and the "terrible- two-year-old"), yet staying within the limits of curriculum or frame of reference.

Changing the focus from ordering students to

learn into letting them choose what (or how) they want to learn unleashes the force for deep learning. Very few of us actually enjoy doing things we are told to do - of course this also depends on the way the order is given, but mostly we want to imagine having free will.

Give well-structured freedom within reasonable limits and watch your class learn this year more than ever!

Big Mistake No 50: Not listening

Tony Blakely
Deputy Head

As a young PE teacher starting at the end of the 70s, my enthusiasm to be a great teacher disabled my ability to be what all great teachers are; a good listener.

I was so full of advice and thought I was so worldly wise (as many 20 something young people think they are) which led to me hearing the start of the problem a pupil was speaking about, then jumping in with sage and erudite solutions.

This, of course, I discovered later, was generally pretty useless and it did take time to understand that often pupils present a concern simply needing a listening post and do not want advice.

I can't say how many years it took to get this right but wish someone had told me at Teacher

Training College. Now, 35 years into my career I am able to advise other colleagues about this really vital part of any teacher's tool kit and would like to think that there are adults out there who remember me as, amongst other things, a teacher who listened and only gave advice when it was right to give it.

Big Mistake No 51: Inflexibility

**Kashmir Sanghera -
Teacher**

Have a flexible consistency of approach when dealing with issues since one size doesn't fit all, but you need to be seen to be fair.

Big Mistake No 52: Forgetting you are human

Vicky Kakos
Primary Classroom Teacher & Educational Psychologist
http://www.in2schools.co.uk

As teachers we are placed on a perfection pedestal by society, our pupils, ourselves or a combination of all three!

My tip is to remember you are only human and to demonstrate this to your students.

Everyone makes mistakes, gets frustrated and has off days… if students observe their teacher being human it makes them much more accessible.

Teachers' failures can provide a valuable lesson for students- by observing how teachers cope when things don't go to plan students can build on their bank of coping mechanisms.

By being human, teachers will also find

themselves in a position where they need to apologise to students- it's inevitable, we can't do everything right by them all the time.

Hearing a teacher say they are sorry can be a powerful moment and can develop a greater level of trust and co-operation between teachers and students.

And remember, if we want students to be sincere when they are apologising, teachers need to be sincere when they are in the wrong too.

Big Mistake No 53: Not Recognising Success

Eilidh Milnes
Speaker

When I was researching material for "Love your Life, Survive the System - a teacher's happiness curriculum, Philip Whiston, a primary teacher turned Staffordshire head teacher, shared these great ideas:

Well done greeting – Be smart with your smartboard!
The idea of a greeting for when the children come in was an idea that was introduced to me via a superb teaching assistant. We use smartboards in every classroom. Frequently these will have a timetable displayed on them. This helps with organisation and adds some structure to the children's day.

A greeting proved to be a more motivational tool. The text would be a celebration of a certain child. Clipart, such as clapping hands or balloons, was added. Text was made colourful, perhaps with some stars around it. It may have been that a certain piece of work stood out. If this was the case a message would be displayed such as: "Well done David for producing a superb piece of work in numeracy. He really understands division now!" Obviously, this worked well for children in need of a confidence boost.

Alternatively, we had the option of displaying group messages such as, "Star group made us all proud by improving their mental arithmetic scores!" Football team successes, netball games and certificates all made their way onto our board. Take care to celebrate improvement as a mark of achievement, rather than high-scores.

Benefits

Class self-esteem increases. We show that we value effort, dedication and improvement. It allows us to make every child feel special. An unforeseen benefit was that the smartboard faced the windows. Parents dropping off children in the morning could also see if their child had been mentioned. They were made aware of how we valued positive contributions and attitude.

Achievement boards – re-cycle the whiteboard

Smartboards are versatile. I do have a large whiteboard along one wall too. We turned this into a powerful tool for positive reinforcement of our school values. A5 sized certificates with smiley faces, rosettes, trophies and the like were printed.

Celebrate!

Every time the children did something of note, we filled out one of these certificates and attached it to the board. We ensured that reasons such as being a good friend, helping someone out when they were struggling in class, sharing, achievement in sport or music, etc were noted, rather than straightforward academic success. This ensured that the children who sometimes do not get full marks could feel equally as valued in class. Improvement was celebrated over high marks.

Refer-a-friend

We developed this idea even further. One of the children asked if they could recommend a friend. This struck me as a superb idea, as peer praise is a powerful a reward. This had the added benefit of creating a good feeling in the class as it fostered class relations. Not all recommendations came from expected sources. Sometimes children got noticed by children they did not previously consider close friends. Any child or adult who visited would be able to view them. Parents during parents' evening were made aware of how we valued success in class. It was always good if they spotted their own child's name in lights.

Big Mistake No 54: Taking All External Criticism On Board

Barry Jackson
Speaker

It happens almost every year. Just after the exam results have been announced, just after the results show higher grades than ever before, someone from the corporate world says something like, "This is all very well but it's about time the education system addressed the qualities that employers are really looking for in candidates." If you're a teacher, this is pretty discouraging. So remember the following, "anyone who is not encouraging you has forfeited the right to influence you" and "don't let the b*****s get to you!"

Nevertheless, there is a serious point here which needs to be addressed and it's a point with a paradox, two paradoxes to be precise. Firstly, schools are doing more than at any time in living memory to prepare students for the world of work. Secondly, they are doing this by involving visiting business people in mock interviews, enterprise events and work experience. If, in spite of this, employers are still not seeing the standard of employability skills they would like, we have to ask why this is and what we can do about it. When business people are going into schools as regularly as they do, it's hardly fair to shovel all the blame onto schools for this sad date of affairs.

What follows is my interpretation of where things are going wrong and what ought to be done about it. I leave you, the teacher to make up your own mind as to whether I'm right or not.

SCHOOL OUTCOMES

The performance of schools, and individual teachers within a school, are measured on exam results. They are not measured according to the future career success of their students. Gloucestershire Federation of Small Businesses has recently suggested that this ought to be a measured outcome for every secondary school though quite how this might work in practice remains a moot point. What seems beyond doubt is that positions in league tables has led to a situation where many schools have become little more than "exam factories." A teacher in one of the Birmingham Grammar schools, who use my services regularly, has told me that, among his own colleagues, there is a division of opinion as to whether visits by local business people represent "curriculum enhancing" or "curriculum interrupting" activities and that opinions on this subject are split pretty evenly. I don't think this school, which is one of the highest performing schools in the country, is atypical. If you're a school head, can you be blamed for deciding that employability skills training needs to be no higher than number 147 on your priority list when half your staff will complain if you interrupt their lessons.

FUNDING

There is, and never has been, funding for schools which is ring fenced for the purpose of developing skills in students which employers value. Until there is, most schools are not going to give this sort of training the priority it deserves. Why should they be expected to do so? I was told recently by a work related learning teacher that she had no budget for this type of training; yet I read in the local paper a fortnight later that the same school had bought brand new lap tops for every single student from year 7 to second year 6th form, over 2,000 lap tops. If I were a parent, concerned about the career prospects of my son or daughter, I would be horrified. But no doubt the salesman who clinched this deal will be holidaying in the Seychelles on the bonus he earned!

Due to government funding cuts, I am coming across schools that are being forced to make staff redundancies to keep within budget. Guess where staff cuts are most likely to fall. Work related learning; and this at a time when unemployment is higher in the 18 to 25 year age group than in any other age bracket. This is frightening, it really is.

UNREALISTIC EXPECTATION

I frequently take part in mock interview events

organised by schools in my area. These are usually well organised and a lot of fun to take part in. At the end of the session, teachers are at pains to tell the interviewers what a great experience it has been and how encouraging the experience was for their students. It gives me a warm fuzzy feeling to receive this kind of feedback; but we have to ask ourselves the brutally honest question, "How valuable is this sort of thing, really?" Let's assume for a moment that the feedback I gave to each student was "top drawer" advice and let's also assume that each student I interviewed was a highly motivated, responsive student who really appreciated the advice I shared. Here's the reality. The mock interview has taken place in year 10 or early in year 11 to avoid the exam period. Assuming the student will leave school after G.C.S.E.'s and join an apprenticeship scheme, it's going to be 12 months, at least, before he has an opportunity to put into practice any of the ideas I shared. If he goes on to study for "A" levels, we can add another 2 years and a further 3 years if he then goes on to university! However good the interviewer, however motivated the student, is it realistic to expect that he will be able to put in to practice anything he was told in a mock interview several years previously? Come on! I'm good but I'm not that good.

As a teacher you don't need to be reminded about the impact Health and Safety and Child Protection legislation has had on work experience. Employers who used to offer work experience are now refusing to do so because of the paper work involved. Those that do continue to offer help in this area are finding themselves more and more restricted in the experience they're allowed to offer. The value to the student in terms of what they learn about the world of work is rapidly diminishing while the time a teacher has to devote to finding places is spiralling out of control.

Then we have "enterprise days." Now, these can be of immense value. I know schools where students have set up real companies, trading real products designed and produced by the students. Fabulous approach. I have also come across events which masquerade as enterprise events but which, in the words of an H.R. Director I talked to, are no more than "play dough exercises." You know the type of thing I mean. Students are given 6 toilet rolls, nine yards of sticky tape, coloured pens and a supply of paper clips and told to build a particle accelerator! At the end of the exercise they are told they have learned the principles of leadership, team work, creativity thinking, design, planning, production and financial control. Have they now? Have they really? And guess who's running these events. Business people! Heaven help us.

LACK OF CONTINUITY
Here, I want to return to the point I made when I talked about the mock interview program. Whatever the exercise involving visiting business people, however relevant the ideas those people share with your students, the reality is that the students are not going have a chance to talk with them ever again. As a teacher, no-one knows better than you do you

that, however well you explain something in the classroom and however responsive and motivated your students may be, there will be things they don't understand, things they simply forget. The sensible student will come to you and say, "Sir, I didn't understand that bit about.......do you mind going over that again with me?" or "Please Miss, you remember what you said last month about......well I've forgotten it. Can you go over it again with me?" And you're delighted to be asked, aren't you? Of course you are. What if a student would like to ask that of the business person who visited the school last month, last year, a couple of years ago?

I decided that I ought to speak to Vanessa Aris about this. For 25 years, Vanessa was career teacher at a private school in Cheltenham. She has been awarded an M.B.E. for her contributions to education. She has told me that, in her opinion, this is the biggest single issue that needs to be put right if schools are going to help students as much as they deserve to be helped. After all, isn't that the way we teach curriculum subjects? Would we even consider getting rid of permanent maths staff because a member of the rotary club, who happens to be a retired maths teacher, offers to visit the school once a year and deliver a maths lesson for free? Hey! There's a G.C.S.E. maths exam next summer. We'd better organise a maths lesson! We would never train a curriculum subject that way. Yet this is how we approach employability training; and then we're surprised when employers are less than impressed with what comes out of the education system.

THE WAY FORWARD
This must all sound pretty negative; and didn't I start by saying that anyone who is not encouraging you forfeits the right to influence you? So here are my suggestions. They may stimulate you to come up with ideas of your own which would work far better in your own school; and that will be a whole lot better than simply adopting my suggestions, right?

• You can't get away from outcomes on which you are going to be measured. There are some priorities which you can't escape even if you wanted to. This does not mean that you can offer your students nothing more. If your school can offer employability training to a standard most schools don't even consider, imagine what a great "selling point" this could be on Parents' Evening.

•   I have written both to the Secretary of
State for Education, Michael Gove, and to the
Chairman of the Commons Select Committee
for Business and Enterprise, Adrian Bailey,
asking them to address the above issues. What
will come of this initiative I have no idea, but
funding is not going to come pouring into
schools any time soon. However, Heads have
more discretion in this area than they care to
admit. The story about the 2,000 lap tops was
just one example I could give you. In most
schools the money is there. Only you can decide
where your priorities lie. If your school is going
for Academy status, you have more room for
manoeuvre than non-academy institutions.

•   Manage your expectations realistically
when you involve local business people. Not all
business people relate equally well to students.
Some do not engage with them at all but talk at
them. Pointless exercises of dubious value,
masquerading as team building, are rife in
industry. Don't be conned into believing that
designing a hadron collider out of elastic bands
and paper clips must be a good idea just
because the person who suggested it was a
business person! Don't be afraid to ask
questions like, "Just what are my students going
to learn from this exercise?" Make them justify

it. Explore the possibility of forming long term partnerships with business people, partnerships which will encourage ongoing contact with students and, if appropriate, their parents as well. This is crucial.

(If you would like a discussion with me, I'm never more than a phone call away)

Big Mistake No 55: Not Getting Students To Help Each Other

Lee Taylor
Stuart Bathurst Catholic High School College of Performing Arts

Day one – you turn up to teach 10Z and you are faced with 32 fifteen year old classroom experts. They have already had 9 full years of education, at least 5 hour per day, 195 days per year which means they has 'enjoyed' 8775 one hour lessons not including tutor time and nursery. They know how to run a class; they have seen the best and worst at it.

Do not teach that class, there is no such thing as a 'class' until you have formed them into a team. Teams of 32 do not work so go for teams of 4 and use a co-operative learning approach.

Utilise all the prior data you have before you meet them and make sure you talk to trusted teachers who already know them. If you go in with a predestined seating plan you will be met with hostility and then spend the next year dreading the lesson and trying to persuade them that you are a human.

Explain what a 'heterogeneous' team is (if you don't know then find out now – no I mean now!) and work with the class to agree a suitable seating plan. It should look like this:

Set-up

Middle-higher ability student	Lower ability student	Pairs are set up as face or shoulder partners so that highest and lowest achievers never work together
Higher ability student	Middle-lower ability student	

Students are numbered to help class and team management. The teacher may set random numbering or predetermine numbers to engineer sub groups

In this way the highest achieving pupil will work with a face or shoulder partner who is near to their own standard but not as a pair with the lowest ability pupil, this would only serve to hold back the fastest learner and demean the slowest learner. Give each team (group is *bad*) a challenge to agree a team name which will go on their books and a team celebration for when they feel successful – it's a rhino thing.

Tell them they must let every person in the team have their own say (round robin) without interruption and then choose one person from each team (give them all a number and pick one number for all of the teams e.g 3) to chair a meeting of their team to agree a consensus about their name and celebration.

Make sure there is a time limit of about four minutes – any longer and you have lost it. Call another number and ask for the name and to see the celebration. By this time they will be having fun and you start to become a cool teacher because you are prepared to listen to them (this is rare in many schools).

Do a class vote on which is the most 'rhino' name and celebration and get them to explain their responses to the class. Set a new task to decide an appropriate reward or recognition for the selected team's success. Discuss this with the class and reach a consensus (I usually get the teams to provide the rewards themselves for the whole class – some teams have become very good at cake making and to be honest, if the pupils are enjoying the lesson and keen to succeed that what is a few crumbs between friends).

Set your classroom out like this:

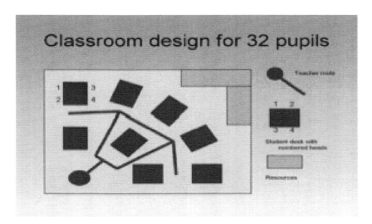

You will be able to get round to each team (you are the visiting 5th member where you will meddle in the middle) and it ensures there is no hierarchy between tables and pupils with a single focus point when you need to chair the class. If white boards and stuff are in the wrong place then get them moved, it is too important not to get things exactly right, you are the impresario of this symphony.

So, there you have it!

How to avoid the 55 BIG mistakes that are costing teachers results, stress and missed opportunities!

Classroom Management Techniques That Work

Do let David know how you have used this book, adapted the content to suit you and the difference it's made.

Being the best you can be, giving 100%, is tiring and at times can mean taking measured risks to get the results that you require.

Mediocrity can be achieved by:

Doing what you have always done, thinking and behaving in the same way............ and then expecting better results

www.stretchdevelopment.com
www.goalsettingaudio.com
http://www.davidhyner.com

David Hyner (fpsa)

12370031R00095

Printed in Great Britain
by Amazon.co.uk, Ltd.,
Marston Gate.